ALL ABOUT
Life

A Black Man's Journey

JOHNNY ALBRITTON JR.

ALL ABOUT
Life

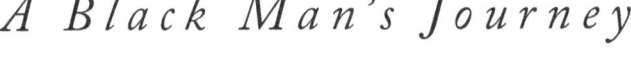

A Black Man's Journey

"Your story is our priority"

LitPrime Solutions
21250 Hawthorne Blvd
Suite 500, Torrance, CA 90503
www.litprime.com
Phone: 1-800-981-9893

Published by LitPrime Solutions   11/16/2023

ISBN: 979-8-88703-297-9(sc)
ISBN: 979-8-88703-298-6(e)

Library of Congress Control Number: 2023916796

I would like to take a couple of minutes of your time to dedicate this book to family and friends. I would like to thank our Heavenly FATHER who gave his only SON(JESUS CHRIST) to die for us that I may have the chance to write this book. GOD gave me the mind and words to write the things that we need daily in our lives to survive on this planet which is constantly at war, not only fighting against each other but the spiritual war fare against good and evil. Thank you FATHER for you holy spirit.

I would like to thank my mother, Mrs. Della Clark for the love that she in still in me and the direction in the path of good. Teaching me to be responsible in what ever I do. My mother not only taught me in words but she is an example of love, patience, and her ultimate goal is to be Godlike in every way possible.

Today she still suggests good advice to me. Once a good mother, always a good mother. I am so very happy that GOD bless me with a wonderful, loving mother. I love you very much(ma).

I was blessed to have two mothers as such. My mother in law, Mrs. Jessie May Batts. My mother in law is no longer alive physically but her kindness and her love is always with me. She always wishes the best for me.

I would like to say that my children are partly responsible for this book. I love all my children very much and I am very proud of them. MY sons, Johnny 111 and Lamar and my daughters Laiquan, Jessica and Sharita. My children to me are as was Joseph was to Abraham. I am so very proud of you all (love daddy).

I am dedicating this book also to all my grandchildren. They are Josiah, Keon, Tamar, and little Reggie, Jaylan, Jalene, Shanice, LaShanda, Kadir and Neveah, Azalea, Zahara, Caleb, Noah, Tagae.

I would like to dedicate this also to my sisters, Zona and Sakalyah(Bettina) whom I love very much.

I really like to dedicate this book to my wife who put up with me as I try to make a difference in my way of life as I live on this earth. She is very patience, just like her mother and she is always there for me. She reads over my work and make very good suggestions. Reba is the other half of my life, that's why she is my wife.

I dedicate this book to every one that reads it and hope that GOD will change your life to be a new creature in him and to renew your spirit within. GOD bless all my family and friends to the up most, I love you all.

Contents

Job the Man

There was a man who lived in the land, who was wealthy as could be,
He obeyed GOD's commands and GOD loved him so because he
    lived righteously,
Job was happy with the accomplishments that he had made in life,
He had seven sons and three daughters and a beautiful wife.
Satan came to GOD and said, "Job your servant has given you his pledge,
But allow me to break him, then he will curse you, but first remove
    your hedge,"
So GOD said go, so Satan took Job's family and even all his wealth,
When Job still gave praises to GOD, Satan asked GOD to allow him
    to take even Job's health,
Now Job is sitting out on the ground with dust upon his head.
Even Job's wife said, "Job curse GOD, you are better off dead,"
Now here comes three of Job's so-called friends,
Saying, "Job, what have you done? Why don't you repent of all of your
    sins?"
Job raised his head and then asked, "How can you speak so bold?
Are you GOD? Were you here? Did you form my soul?"
Job says, "how I long for the months gone by, for the days when GOD
    watched over me,
When his beautiful lamp shone upon his head and even down to his feet,
And by his light I walk through darkness down here on this earth,

Oh, how I long for the days when I was in my prime, GOD has been
   with me from my birth.
When I went to the gate of the city and took my seat in the square,
All would come around me when they knew I was there,
The young men saw me and stepped aside and the old men rose to
   their feet,
The chief men refrained from talking when they heard me begin to
   speak.
Those who knew me spoke well of me, because I rescued the poor,
Those that were fatherless and them that cried out for help, to these I
   gladly opened my door,
I was eyes to the blind and feet to the lame, and I was a father to the
   needy,
I took up the case of the stranger and I rebuked the greedy.
Now they all mock me young and old of any race,
When they see me now, they do not hesitate to spit in my face,
Night pierces my bones, my gnawing pains never rest,
Oh GOD, I cried out, is this what I get for doing my best?
Is it not ruin for the wicked, disaster for those who do wrong?
Does not GOD see my ways and count my every step, oh GOD, is
   this where I belong?
Oh that I had someone to hear me, and let my accuser put his indictment
   in writing,
I would give him an account of every step and ask of him why with
   me is he fighting?
I could never put my trust in gold or in fortune my hands had gained,
For I dread destruction from GOD and for fear of his splendor, I could
   do no such things,"
Job showed himself righteous before his three friends, they had no more
   to say or nothing else to do,
So another voice came forward, a young man named Elihu.
"I've sat here long enough, I waited while you spoke,
Therefore I say listen to me, I too will tell you what I know."
Elihu said, "Listen, Job, I am perfect in knowledge to a peak. "

After Elihu finished, the Lord Almighty said, "Now I am going to speak."

The Lord said to Job, "Brace yourself like a man, I will question you,

What part of creating the world and of man and the animals did you have to do?"

After the Lord had finished questioning Job about the earth and nature's plan,

Job said, "I'm sorry, Lord, I spoke of things I did not understand.

My ears had heard of you, but now my eyes have seen you,

Therefore I despise myself and repent in dust and ashes, this I do."

Then the Lord said to Job's friends, "Your words came out of nowhere,

In order for me to forgive you, you must ask Job to pray for you, then I will accept his prayer.

After Job prayed, he was made prosperous again, twice as much as before,

Just you remember what Job went through when trouble knocks at your door,

It may seem like GOD has abandoned you,

Just remember he is there, waiting to see which road you will choose.

Jesus

to make you gay when you are burdened,
And to make you gayer when you are gay,
Just sing, and say praises to Jesus every minute, every hour, every day.

Five Senses

I hear:
The wind that my GOD causes to blow.
I see:
The nature that my GOD causes to grow.
I feel:
The warmth and the cold my GOD causes to come and go.
I smell:
The fragrances of the flowers of the summer and in the winter of snow.
I taste:
The goodness of my GOD in some of the places I know.
But yet with these same eyes, I see the world in desperate need of my
    Lord.
Also smelling the filthiness and uncleanliness of this world.
At the same time tasting the bitterness and hatred of this world,
But GOD still gives me the love and that warm feeling to work for
    him in this world.

We Know Not the Time

No man knows when his time will come,
When all his loving and his work down here on this earth will be done,
As a fish that has been caught in a cruel net,
And as a special trap that has just been set,
Or as a bird that has just been taken in a snare,
You know not your time, you could be anywhere,
We could be at work or just going out to play,
We could be visiting a friend or taking a walk, all on a routine day,
We could be in a church or just picking up some food from the store,
We could be just driving along or vacationing at a beautiful resort,
Just remember don't wait, because it might be too late,
Only what you do for the Lord will last,
Everything else is vanity and will surely pass.

Which One Is Right?

There are so many different beliefs today,

They all believe that theirs is the right way,

the Witnesses believe that they have the one hundred and forty-four
thousand amongst them you see,

While the Adventist says keeping the Sabbath is the most important
command to me,

On the other hand, you have the Muslims who teach,

That Jesus was just another prophet and that black people we need to
reach,

the Baptists believe as long as they go to church and have a good time,

Praising the name of Jesus not realizing that the sin in our lives must
be put far behind,

The Catholics want to control all the world's religions under one power,

They have lowered their standards, to lead more people astray in this
earth's last hour,

The Sanctify and Holy go all day dancing and shouting and speaking
in tongues you must possess,

If you do not then the spirit on you it did not rest,

Then we have all different groups which are classified as occult,

Some believe in racism, while others indulge in free sex to male to male
and children to adults,

The lust of the flesh has taken over the whole corrupt world and in the
churches has worked its way,

All the preachers and teachers and even the Pope see this and have
    nothing to say,
People steal, kill, fornicate, and take drugs all through the week,
Sabbaths and Sundays the same one you will find in church their Lord
    trying to seek,
There are some who want to walk that long narrow road,
    but just honestly don't know how,
To them I say fall down on your knees and seek the Lord right now,
Pray for forgiveness of your sins and ask for the Holy Spirit to guide,
You in truth and give you wisdom, knowledge, and understanding as
    the Bible you open wide,
Jesus said that there is only one GOD, one baptism and only one Spirit
    on which we must rely,
On all these others no matter how right they seem we must not try,
There is only one true church and they who love the Lord with all their
    heart and keep his commands,
And drive out all sin from one's life and put all your trust and hope in
    GOD and not in man.
So there it is people, now you know it's hard work,
Only them that studies GOD's word and love and obeys can be in his
    true church,
It's not a building down here on this earth built by human hands,
It's only them who worship GOD and his Son in spirit can understand,
The promises of GOD we can really claim,
What He did for David, Moses, and Job for us he will do the same,
Study and show thyself approved, we were told,
Commit yourself to GOD and don't give yourself to the devil just to
    be sold,
Jesus, GOD's only Son, has already paid the price,
When He hung between heaven and earth for us to make it right,
Now do you see as you look at these religions, down here on this earth,
They all are from man's hand that gave them birth,
Some will ask now, what will I do if I don't go to church anymore
    with them,

Remember Jesus said where two or more that are gathered in my name,
    there I am with him,
With him, because they are on one accord, you see,
Just praising and honoring GOD for his grace and his goodness and
    his strength he is giving to you and me.

Psalm 1

Blessed is the man who does not walk with the wicked or Stand with
    the sinners or sit with the mockers at their table.
But his delight is in the law of the Lord, and he meditates
Day and night, which makes him strong and able,
To be like a tree planted by streams of water, which yields its fruit in
    season,
Whose leaf does not wither, when asked why he gives
GOD as his only reason,
Whatever he does shall prosper, but GOD only has that say,
Not so the wicked! They are like the chaff that the wind will blow away.
Therefore the wicked will not stand in the judgment, nor sinners in
    the assembly of those who do right,
For the Lord watches over the way of the righteous, but The way of the
    wicked will perish from God's sight.

Depression

Everyone is complaining how hard times are today
Trying to live a decent life with all these high taxes to pay
People are scared of how bad things are which have some gun-packing
Never knowing while you are out you may be the next
victim of a carjacking
So many people are without someone to comfort them in times of need
When a best friend is very sick or a loved one that passed is very hard
    to believe
I must say that the dead who had already died
Are better off than the living who are still alive,
But better than both is he who has not yet been,
Born in this evil, sick, degenerate world full of immorality and sin.

What is Thy Name?

Man wants to know thou holy name
The Jews call you Yahweh, some say Jehovah means the same
Jesus told me to call you Father you see
Because Jesus said, "You loved me so much you sent him to die for me."
You see, Heavenly Father, I know your name, you told us
But still I feel so much better and closer to you when I call you my
      Father, in whom I put all my trust.

Chasing After the Wind

What does a man gain from all his labors?
Is it for his family or trying to keep up with his neighbors?
We work very hard to save a little and pay our bills,
Just when you think you are a little ahead of the game,
Something else comes up to set you back still.
Just as the sun rises and the sun sets,
Early in the morning we go to work and in the evening we come home,
    what do we get?
Babies are born almost every minute, this I can't deny,
While at the same time somewhere in the world someone will die.
We fill our gas tanks only for the gas to be used up again,
All is vanity, chasing after the wind,
The more knowledge man thinks he knows,
The more trouble and grief for mankind grows.
And yet when I stop and look at all of this, that's going on under the sun,
We aren't doing anything new that hasn't already been done,
So what is man's purpose here on earth? I wish it could be understood,
Just to live to eat and drink and try to do good?
If that is what you are thinking, my friend, you are just chasing after
    the wind, that's no doubt.
Man was created here to know and serve the Almighty GOD
And from his life, drive all evil out,

Man is made from the dust of the earth and to the dust he must return,
The righteous are saved and the wicked will bum,
All is vanity, vanity, when chasing after the wind,
Give up the chase, my friend, and to GOD go in.

How Much Do They Cost?

Man digs mines for silver and gold,
After they are refined, then they are sold.
Iron is taken from the earth and copper is smelted from ore,
We purchase merchandise made of these materials from the store.
Man pays billions to go to the moon,
Now they will pay even more to try to get to Mars soon.
Man tunnels through rock to the center of the earth far beyond our sight,
Then from the darkest part of the earth, he brings up many strange
    and hidden things to light.
He also goes deep, deep to the deepest part of the ocean floor,
He keeps on going until the great ocean pressure forbids him to go
    no more.
But where can wisdom be found and where does understanding dwell?
These are they that man can never price to sell.
They could never be bought with all the silver and gold on this earth,
Because man will never comprehend its real worth.
They are priceless! Man asks where can they be found?
So he continues his search from town to town.
Man who relies on man, will never think of
To find wisdom and understanding you go to GOD up above.
GOD understands the way to it and He alone knows where they dwell,
For He views the ends of the earth and sees everything under the
    heavens as well.

When He established the forces of the wind and measured out the
waters above and below,
Then He made a decree for the rain and a path for the thunderstorm,
only He can know.
Then GOD says to man, "You ask me where are they, how much do
they cost and are they not demanding?"
GOD says, my son, the fear of the Lord, that is wisdom and to shun
evil that is understanding.

I Can't Do It Alone

Please Holy Spirit come into my life
Remove the evil spirit of hatred and strife
Comfort me and hold me as I seek thy way
Guide my feet and control my tongue and hold my hand every day.
I seek to do the will of my Father above
To study the word and live it out in love
I really love you Holy GOD and Jesus your son
For everything you show me and for all that you have done.
You guide me through your word so plain
Why can't others see if it's not from you GOD it's all in vain
I feel so lonely and lost when I'm not in your word
I feel like a lonely, flying, lost little bird.
Thank you, Holy Spirit, for coming into my life
Thank you, my GOD, for bringing me out of darkness into the light
My GOD, the truth is so very bright.

A Prayer for Mankind

There was a man who went down to Alabama and Tennessee
To tell the white people to let his people be
There were some who didn't want to do this thing
So instead, they shot and killed Dr. Martin Luther King.
Even today, as we can plainly see
People are still blind of letting others be free
Even though we really don't know who shot Dr. King
But we can be sure on one important thing.
That is, when they assassinated Dr. King, they didn't think of
There was someone watching them, that's my Lord above
They may escape from people down here on this earth
But they can't escape from the one who gives and takes away births.
We all know Dr. King wanted equality and peace
So why can't we let all this racial fighting cease?
Even though we have all these racial problems from land to land
I can say honestly that I am not prejudiced against any man.
We have these groups called the Muslims and the Ku Klux Klan
They both say they are doing right but to me they are making it more
    difficult for the survival of man
My Lord, people here on earth go about solving problems any old kind
    of way
But if they only knew the answer, that is, to obey you and fall on their
    knees and pray.

If all people of all races could see this way is best
I am sure, Lord, we all would see a great deal of progress
Oh, Lord, I feel so bad about the death of Dr. King inside
But from what I see this feeling is nationwide.
But in spite of the way the people feel
Will that dream of our Dr. King really become real?
Oh Lord, I know some people of all races want to do their best
So Father, give them the desire to ask for forgiveness.
Oh Lord, I know some people are stubborn and weak and can't get along
But Heavenly Father, I pray for them to make their love for you and
    mankind spiritually strong
Father we go to church to praise you and sing
But Father, may I ask of you just one more thing?
Please forgive us all for what we have done
Father, let us all want to live as equally as one.

What Happened to Justice?

Whatever happened to the old way of the law that used to be clean,
Today's justice is the worst I have ever seen,
A white man is innocent until proven guilty of a crime,
Whereas a black man is guilty, trying to prove his innocence while
    already serving his time.
Even our judges we can't trust to be impartial to a case until the facts
    are heard,
The prejudiced lawyers will tell you don't believe what you see, just
    listen to my words.
Your eyes are deceiving, not worth believing, but I can point out to
    you the facts,
"They shouldn't have done this or been there or said this, or maybe
    because they are just blacks."
It's really a shame, that the crime is not the blame, that the Court of
    Law is supposed to listen for,
But rather they support their own personal view that white is right and
    sweep the black innocents right through a jail cell door,
The law says I am not supposed to prove my innocence as you say,
Do your job, man and try to prove that I am guilty. Why don't you
    really earn your pay?
Oh the media! Don't even believe what they say or print,
They are just trying to get a high rating or a big sell,
Their chief editor is Satan, the father of lies, remember
He's the one who's going to be in charge of hell.

Remember

Remember way back in those olden days
When our parents and grandparents used to be slaves
Remember when they all knew how to treat one another?
They had respect for the sister and love for the brother
Even though every day was tough
They still stayed together even when times were rough.
Mr. Charlie couldn't understand what it was that kept them together
  and made them strong
But the secret was prayer and singing praises to the Lord all the day long
Now that time has changed to where we are supposed to be free
Many blacks have lost that love for the brother and for the sister, they
  lost that courtesy.
Now we are in the age of the Black and Proud
We say black is beautiful and we say it loud
Now we walk around just a little big bigger
Wanting to be called Black and dared to be called a nigger.
Now since we have grown out of childhood and toys
Since we are young men now, don't treat us like or call us boys
Remember the thing that has been said, we must all take this in
That when we are taken advantage of, it's usually the brother with the
  same color skin.
So this shows me that our parents of old were sort of alright

Because today we have not only the white man but our own people
    to fight
Black, red, and white are just skin color names
But remember in GOD's sight we are all the same.
So when we see Jesus coming in the clouds for the victory which will
    be won!
He will be gathering all those who worked, worshipped, and loved one
    another as one
So people of all, remember as we depart
With Jesus, it's not the color of your skin but what's in your heart.

The Time Machine

Yesterday I was seventeen and asking my father for the keys to his car
I woke up the next day and I am fifty-seven and wondering where my keys are
Only yesterday I was teaching my son how to throw and catch a baseball
today he has a family and a good job and he will be graduating from college this fall
Yesterday we took all the children to the zoo and had a lot of fun
The next day I am watching my child on television, watching how fast she can run
Only yesterday I was just teaching her how to ride her bike, jump rope, and play jacks
Seems like a couple of weeks later she has grown up now and has life on the right tracks
Life itself is a time machine, if one would closely observe
Only yesterday my wife had those knockout body curves
I had the body of a muscleman and ran every day to keep my body in tune
Yes that was only yesterday, but today I can hardly work out, maybe twice last June
When our youngest daughter was about three years old, she would always say
Daddy, I don't want to ever grow up I want to stay small always

That was just only yesterday, now today she is all grown up and moved
away
Tears come to my eyes when I think of all the past and where it has gone
How fast time for me is starting to end my life song
Life is a time machine that no man can ever control
Learn to appreciate your family every day, because today you will be
young and tomorrow you will be old.

What's Going On?

Man, somebody tell me what is going on with the people today
I remember when I was a kid in my house the father had the last say
I remember when the kid did not participate in an adult conversation
I couldn't even be in the same room, if I did I would experience
    devastation
Talking back to my parents wasn't even an option that was a task that
    was much too large
Today the children control the parents and run the household like they
    are in charge
Man, somebody tell me what is going on with the people today
Men are raping children and don't care how young they may be
They could be fifteen years old or as young as a child the age of three
Now I know back in the day when I was a kid, those things you didn't
    get away very far
Then the mothers were real mothers and the fathers found you no
    matter where you are
You just didn't mess with children in your right mind unless you were
    on drugs
Brother back there in those days it didn't matter what your excuse was
Today they say he had no childhood or they were abused when they
    were small
How can you even attempt to find an excuse for a man two hundred
    and twenty pounds and six feet tall?

Man, somebody tell me what is going on with the people today

Mothers are killing their own children for money, to be with another
or just plain tired

The lawyers will try to find excuses for this one so they can get hired

These lawyers will tell you anything if you give them the floor

They will have you believing that the kid or kids were the cause of the
kid's head slamming into the door

These so-called mothers protect their men and turn on their own
children in a court of law

Just to get what they call love from a child molester, but the love of a
mother the children never saw

I have seen them come on national television and know they are lying

About their child is missing even after they participated and watched
their children dying

Man, somebody tell me what is going on with the people today

Someone needs to speak up about our law enforcement officers in the
way they serve

They are taking advantage of the uniform of which they do not deserve

They are evil and they are racist in their own way, which they attempt
to hide

They will beat you and demoralize you and violate you and try to take
away your pride

They are humans too and they need a lot of help and need not be on
the streets

We already have the robbers, rapists, drug addicts, drunk drivers, and
men who love women to beat

You see we need help when we call 911, not more problems to be
escalated

So have real law enforcement officers who will serve and protect the
violated

Man, somebody tell me what is going on with the people today

I know the future don't look too good and it looks like all the do-good
people are gone

Don't give up hope, my people, don't let the evil in this world steal
your song

Hold on to your good teachings in your personal life as you walk along
this earth

Help others to have a dream and a song in their hearts that they may
teach little ones at birth

So what's going on with the people today, we are all selfish and have
gone our separate ways.

Who Did That?

I keep hearing the phrase: you better take time to smell the roses
How can I, as a photographer, every day I am taking hundreds of poses
Every day people are running here and there and everywhere
Not noticing the beauty all around them, who really cares?
People fly around the world on so-called business trips
Their only goal is about getting paid and not paying
    attention to the beautiful snow capped mountain tips
Only wondering when and how long will we get there soon?
While all the time flying in the beautiful light of the starry sky and
    midnight moon
Business people with their laptop fighting for the goal that must be reached
Ignoring the sound of the waves as they sit on the beautiful white-
    sanded beach
Sometimes we just can't understand what went wrong
I spent all day and I worked so hard all night long
I still didn't meet that quota that was set
Or why didn't I get that position, I was supposed to have been next
One night while outside looking up into the starry sky with my little girl
She said, Daddy how can we go into space? I said we are already on
    this world
I never realized it before now, that we are already in space
I don't need no rocket, GOD has given all of us an ideal place
To watch the skyshow every night and you don't have to pay

The stars, moon, clouds and the galaxies are all there on display
If you listen clearly at night you can hear GOD's creatures
During the day you can see their many different features
Look at those beautiful trees and flowers of so many kinds
The red maples, big oaks, palm trees and those tall magnificent pines
I am so glad I had that talk with my little girl
I don't only smell the roses now but I thank GOD every day and night
    for this beautiful world

If We Are That Bad!

If we are so immoral and so much of nothing that you don't want us
    in your sight
Then why did you put us in slavery to make this land that you live in a delight
You hate us so much that you tried to hang us all until it was a bore
But still you need our bravery to fight all your little dirty wars
We are supposed to be so dirty in your sight
But yet you need us to clean and cook for you day and night
Since we are so uneducated and don't know nothing
Why do you have us raising and teaching your children something?
I am really waiting for a worthwhile answer from you, what do you
    have to say?
Let me tell you something, mister, our blood, sweat and tears built
    this US of A
It's sad when a prisoner of war can eat in a restaurant in the States
When a black man in uniform goes to the same restaurant and gets
    turned away
One with common sense would not drink a glass of poison, they would refuse
You make us feel that we are nothing because of slavery but that was
    just a way to use
Our knowledge, our bravery, our usefulness, our means to survive
And our steadfastness and our faith in GOD that keeps us alive
So, if we are that bad just leave us alone
Because mister, we can do very well on our own

Opportunity

I know you pass all kinds of laws to hold me back
You play with my mind, so I can feel that I wish I wasn't black
You make it almost impossible for me to get a loan
If I do get it you make the interest so high that I will never own
I just know I am not that dumb that I cannot comprehend
I know and you know that you don't want me to know that I can hang in
I can get the job done just as good without all these computer tools
You know that I am born with the knowledge and I am not a fool
But if one brainwashes another long enough through the years
Then one might just about turn all his dreams into fears
We don't want from your money or anything else you see
Just don't close the door on us to the simple opportunity
It's not that you are giving us anything that we don't already deserve
Are you that scared of us that you can't ever throw a straight ball, all
     you have are curves
Well, let me give you something to think about
We are in the bottom of the ninth inning and we are ahead and your
     time is running out
One more thing for anyone who plays a foolish game as such, your life
     will plunder
Just don't you ever forget what GOD has for you no man can put asunder

Why You?

Why do you have all the so-called knowledge of everything?
Why do you think you are the only one with a song to sing?
Why do you think you have all the answers that are needed?
Why do you want everyone to always have to come to you, aren't you
     kind of conceited?
How did you get to be in charge of almost everything in this world?
You make it hard for others but for your kind you always get the pearls
Why do you think everything you do is alright?
How can you think you are right when you are full of darkness and
     know nothing about the light?
While in darkness everything is turned around in reverse
Right is wrong and darkness is light and sin is not a curse
You go to church and pray to GOD, wait a minute, that's odd
If you had eyes to see, this cannot be, because GOD lives in me
If you pray to The GOD that is above
Then clearly you should know that GOD is Love
But how can you see if you are always in the dark?
Maybe try reaching out, you may find that it's not that far
You may just grab someone's hand who can lead you out
Of the life of darkness and to Our GOD, where there is no doubt
Sin has neither color nor nationality
Sin has no life but always wants immortality
Sin was defeated long ago by GOD's only Son

We are its victim, but if we accept His only Son, then we become one
With Him and the Father, now the battle in our lives can be won
You see with the Father and the Son, there is no more I but now it is We
In darkness we were blind but in the true light now we see

A Tribute to Women

The love of a mother that she so tenderly nurtures in her son
Is the love that nothing in this world can cause him to wander
From her dreams that she has for his long life journey ahead
That he will succeed in this evil world in spite of all its bloodshed
Hoping that he will always keep her in his mind in all his decisions
Knowing that one day he will have his own dreams and follow his
    own visions
She also knows how hard it is out on your own, trying to live a good life
Praying to GOD every day and night that he will find a very good wife
As he reflects on his mother and all that she means to him and his welfare
He thanks her every day for her love and all the ways she shows that
    she cares
Today her son has a lot to be thankful of, not only a dedicated mother
    but a beautiful wife and girl twins to love
But he gives thanks every day and night to his GOD above
His wife's mother is the second mother in his life who loves him very much
He knows he is blessed when he has three good women in his life they touch
His very soul, encouraging him that he can do and achieve his highest goal
Now, he has his own business and their dream house without selling
    his soul
He learned the lessons of life by listening to his mother, he dedicated
    his love to his wife by not loving another
Young men of all ages, if anything in life you must always do

Love your mother and your wife or wife-to-be as they love you
You will find that they are not at all perfect
But regardless, they are due your respect
It is said that man is the head so use it instead
Try love, it is really easier to spread

I Just Came to Say Thank You

Lord I know every time that I come to you, I am always asking for
    something
Every day and every night I am on my knees always really about nothing
Seems like there is always something I want you to do
Always wanting this or please take care of that you know that this is true
Yet you just keep on giving your sovereign love to me every day
You gave me everything when you sacrificed your son for us all I must say
Now I know why you want us to have children to raise up as our own
Because as we teach them and admonish them it will change our tone
One day my daughter kept on begging for something from me
I said dear little girl you have everything you need, can't you see?
You have many things some are old and many are new
You can take the time to ask me for things but never have the time to
    say thank you
As soon as those profound words left my lips and floated in the air
I realized that I am the one who really doesn't care
I am the one who always has a list for my GOD to do
But when was the last time I just took the time to say thank you?
Not only for all the miracles in my life and my family too
But just for the very act of waking me up every morning and being
    clothed in my right mind
Just knowing how much you love us and watch over us all the time

You are interested in the smallest things in our lives and even to the biggest that it can get

You treat them all the same because to you all of them are important and you never forget

How I now come to you knowing that you know what I already need from day to day

I know you told us to still ask, which I do, but much less I am very happy to say

I learned now that when I come I come with a much different tune

I come asking less but now I come to commune

I just want to talk to you GOD and thank you for my day no matter how it turns out

I just want to thank you GOD not only in words but in my daily life as I go about

They have a saying that our children are our echoes and they are our reflections

My GOD after raising them and admonishing them to go into the right directions

I can see myself much more clearly now as you would see me

I must ask Father why you sacrificed so much to set me free?

Then in your words you so calmly say son I love you, a love that will last eternally

While the tears run down my face as they so often do

Because now when I come I am coming most of all to say thank you

Reba

Happy Mother's Day to my dear wife
I love you not only on this day but every day of your life

I have loved you before a mother you became
Today even more special, I love you the same

Since you have become a mother, time just isn't there
For you and me to have a private moment together that our love we
    can share

But just you remember that I love you so
That no one or nowhere else with my love I will go

My GOD says to love you no matter what state we are in
When we are happy or sad, for richer or poorer, our Godly love can
    keep us from sin

I know at times I am not what I am supposed to be
I know sometimes you feel so very, very lonely

Due to the pressures of this life I almost can pop
It's worth it when I know you really love me a lot

I have to dig deep into the storehouse of GOD to get
All that he promised me that I can live a life that I won't have to regret

All your dreams that you wish would come true
Is one of my goals in life to fulfill just for you

I really truly love you as my lover, my friend, and especially as my wife

Remember my love for you on each Mother's Day is my promise to love
you for the rest of your life.

Love, Johnny

Addiction

Mister alcohol, what can you do for me?
Instead of getting me so high that I can't really see.

I can get rid of all that misery and pain that you are in,
Even though all the odds are against you, I can make you feel that you
    can still win.

But Mr. Alcohol, that is just a feeling on which I must not rely.
Oh shut up, boy! Get the bottle and give me a try.

Wait a minute, how about that disease of which you are a free giver.
I think it's the disease called psoriasis of the liver.

Forget about that and concentrate on the good:
I can make you feel just the way you really should.

Mr. Alcohol, Mr. Alcohol, how long will that feeling last?
Just long enough, long enough for the situation to pass.

Mr. Alcohol, there's a question that is bothering me, answer it truthfully:
If I try you, will I be able to face reality?

Of course not, my son, I am just for fun.

I am not made to last, I am a phony, hiding behind reality's mask.

I am very sorry you asked me that question, young man, because Mr. Cigarette and Mr. Drug can't take their stand.

You see, since you introduced us to Mr. Reality,

We now realize that there is nothing that we can do to set a bound man free.

Thank you Mr. Drug and· Mr. Cigarette and a special thank you, Mr. Alcohol.

I made my decision not to drink, because if I do I can't really think.

I don't even want to take a smoke.

What is it really worth to my body, so it must be a joke.

I even don't want to take drugs or take a pill, for all these things come under a satanic will.

For if I do those things, I am like in a prison cell.

Anyway, I want my body and mind to be physically and spiritually well.

So people of all ages, I hope you understand,

If you smoke, drink or take drugs, it doesn't make you more of a woman or a man.

Matter of fact, if you do, it will make you less than what GOD made you.

Jesus, doesn't want you to be as though you are living in a prison for eternity,

Jesus died so that you don't have to do these things and if you are, that you can be free.

It's Time

For those of you who know the truth:
It's time to stop preaching at one another, but it's time to start teaching others.

For those who aren't hot or cold:
It's time in your life to stop playing and now is the time for fasting and praying.

For those of you who love to gossip:
It's time to stop interfering and stop talking. It's time to pick up GOD's word and start walking.

For those whose eyes are closed spiritually:
It's time to stop sleeping, because there will be a time for gnashing of the teeth and weeping.

For those of you who love to say do this and go there:
It's time to stop showing, but as leaders, it's time to start doing.

For those of you who rely on their own understanding:
It's time to stop being confused, but give our hearts and minds to GOD, for him to use.

For those of you who are supposed to be so strong in the faith:
It's time for you to stop condemning the weak, but for you to show a
Christ-like character by being meek.

For those of you who aren't doing anything:
It's time to stop scattering, now as the world is near its end, it's time
to start gathering.

For those of you who aren't sure about something:
It's time for you to stop guessing. Now is the time to ask GOD for
wisdom, knowledge, and understanding, so to others you may be
a blessing.

For those of you who say, I can live my life any old kind of way:
It's time to know about GOD's only Son who He sacrificed for you and
really understand it. Then you will know what Jesus meant when
he said, "If you love me, keep my commandments."

Always Complaining

It's just too hot is all I hear, now that summertime has appeared
Can't you understand that summertime brings on the heat?
You move to Florida to escape the cold and the snow that gets very deep
Then up north you were too cold and always freezing
Now in the south you are too hot or you are always sneezing
When it rains to you the weather is bad
Unless it's a sunny and warm day you are complaining and very sad
You should be glad no matter what the weather brings, my friend
When it rains be glad that you can feel it and that you are not six feet
    deep in
The ground below where no one knows anything
Just think of this, if you were, you wouldn't be able to complain
So be very careful from now on with the words that come from your heart
You never know when they just may be your last and this world you
    will depart.

Money

You will be the one everyone will pick
You get more respect by having a lot of it
You most likely won't go to jail
You most likely will go to hell
You will always be able to pay your bills
All your relatives want to be in your will
The ones with it think they are better than you
Always want to be waited on, like you have nothing else to do
With all that money you should know how to dress
The way you match your clothes is a mess
People with money, seems like they want to move south
Spend your money wisely and you won't have dreams that you will run out
Why does your attitude have to change?
No more smiles, always uptight, man your life is strange
Everyone you meet don't want your money
Just maybe you have more to offer that is sweeter than honey
Did your money replace your family that once was above?
How sad, you know money just can't buy love
Money can't put its arms around you to hold
It may buy you a lot but not youth when you get old
Yes I admit your money made you very wealthy
I don't have much, but I am very healthy
I didn't spend my youth running after it

Now that you are older you have to call it quits
All that time spent to get where you are
Sacrificed your family whom are gone very far
From your lack of interest and don't care way of life
Causing no one wanting to be around you and your strife
If you had it all over to do again
Would you be rich or just plain?
Some people have all the money in the world
They are so mixed up they are getting changed from a boy to a girl
If your goal is money and nothing else is put above
Then money is your only hope and is your only love
I don't envy you, well maybe just a little
Money would ease the pain
I just don't want to go insane
Thinking about all my money some day I will lose
Not knowing that one day I will have to choose
Between my money and my soul it seems
Thank GOD I am just poor and all of this was just a dream.

Can You See?

Can you see what you are doing to me?
When you put yourself way above me
What makes you think that you are all that
Who gave you the keys to life to open all the doors?
Now you think you can tell who goes in?
Not by qualification but by the color of their skin
You know you were not born like that
You were taught to be a person just like that one who taught you
We were made to live with one another believe it or not
Actually we are all from the same person from the beginning of time
But as you know now somehow we all have different clocks
I guess that is why we have wars after wars after wars
Some just can't accept that we all are not the same
All do not have blue eyes and blonde hair
But I know that we all need only to be treated fair
How can one expect you to get along with others
When you can't even get along with your own selves?
How can one expect you to love others
When you can't find it in your heart to even love GOD?
How can one expect you to get respect when you don't respect yourself?
You are constantly looking over your shoulders, I wonder why?
Maybe your conscience knows everything you have stolen
I have many faces and many colors and you say you can't remember me?

I am the one you took from Africa, and I am the one you took to the
    reservation
I am the one you had assassinated and I am the one you had crucified
Well, there seems to be a whole list of "I am the one."
All this I know you just couldn't have been born with, but well taught
Well, there seems to be a whole list of "I am the one."
All this I know you just couldn't have been born with, but well taught
Sorry no excuses here today. You are not a child no more, but a man
If that is what you want to call yourself, of course men or should I say
Real men don't hate, rape, beat women, abuse children in anyway, steal
    from old people,
Sell drugs to children, defend that which is wrong, don't apologize,
    lazy, living on their parents, using their girlfriend's car to see other
    girls, disrespect their parents or anyone else's parents, kill just for
    fun, drink and drive, don't care about what is right and what is
    wrong and finally you may have been rejected by GOD Himself.
You know some things you just can't teach a person
The wrong things that one learns as a child, now that I've become a
    real man
I put away childish things
See no excuses for being useless
You aren't better than me, you are just plain stupid
You know some things can be inherited
That is why it is so important for us to know who our father is
The big question is, is it Satan or is it JEHOVAH GOD?

A Change Will Come

A change must come without all this drama
A change will come in the person of Obama
A change must come as we all can see
A change must come I am sure we all can agree
A change must come but it has to start with me
A change will come as I grasp hold to responsibility
A change will come as I take charge of my family
A change will come when I learn to love
A change will come when I ask for help from above
A change will come when I learn to refuse
A change will come when I cease to excuse
A change will and must come into my life
A change will come when I remove all this strife
A change must come of which I need right now
A change will come if you just show me how
A change will come when we can finally realize
A change will come when we all can reach for the prize
A change will come when everything doesn't have to be just for me
A change will come when I can for others see
A change has come out warily from within
A change has come when we all see the same color skin
A change will come it might take awhile
A change can come now with just a little smile

A change will come for some are glad
A change is inevitable which makes some very mad
A change will show how some people mentally are sick and sad
A change is coming with or with out you so keep up the pace
A change is coming now changing the attitude of this human race
A change has come that might be heavenly sent
A change will come when Obama is elected president.

www.ingramcontent.com/pod-product-compliance
Lightning Source LLC
Chambersburg PA
CBHW020343130626
46549CB00003B/1263